D1544559

A Career in Environmental Engineering

Stuart A. Kallen

ReferencePoint
Press®

San Diego, CA

© 2019 ReferencePoint Press, Inc.
Printed in the United States

For more information, contact:
ReferencePoint Press, Inc.
PO Box 27779
San Diego, CA 92198
www.ReferencePointPress.com

LIBRARY OF CONGRESS CATALOGING-IN-PUBLICATION DATA

Names: Kallen, Stuart A., 1955– author.
Title: A Career in Environmental Engineering/by Stuart A. Kallen.
Description: San Diego, CA: ReferencePoint Press, Inc., [2019] | Series:
  Careers in Engineering | Includes bibliographical references and index.
Identifiers: LCCN 2017054539 (print) | LCCN 2018000316 (ebook) | ISBN
  9781682823521 (eBook) | ISBN 9781682823514 (hardback)
Subjects: LCSH: Sanitary engineering—Vocational guidance—Juvenile
  literature. | Environmental engineering—Vocational guidance—Juvenile
  literature.
Classification: LCC TD156 (ebook) | LCC TD156 .K35 2019 (print) | DDC
  628.023—dc23
LC record available at https://lccn.loc.gov/2017054539

CONTENTS

Environmental Engineering at a Glance 4

Introduction 5
Engineering Everything

Chapter One 8
What Does an Environmental Engineer Do?

Chapter Two 17
How Do You Become an Environmental Engineer?

Chapter Three 24
What Skills and Personal Qualities
Matter Most—and Why?

Chapter Four 31
What Is It Like to Work as an
Environmental Engineer?

Chapter Five 38
Advancement and Other Job Opportunities

Chapter Six 45
What Does the Future Hold for
Environmental Engineers?

Chapter Seven 51
Interview with an Environmental Engineer

Source Notes 54

Find Out More 57

Index 59

Picture Credits 63

About the Author 64

ENVIRONMENTAL ENGINEERING AT A GLANCE

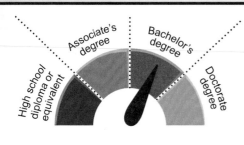

Educational Requirements
Bachelor's degree and above

Certification and Licensing

Professional engineer license (voluntary)

Working Conditions

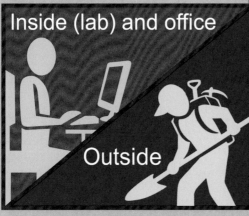

Inside (lab) and office

Outside

Personal Qualities

- ✓ Creative
- ✓ Strong math and science abilities
- ✓ Technical expertise
- ✓ Communication skills
- ✓ Team player

Median pay in 2016   **$84,890**

55,100
Number of jobs as of 2014

Growth rate through 2024

12%

Future Job Outlook

Engineering Everything

Marc Edwards might be one of the world's most famous environmental engineers. In 2015 Edwards was contacted by citizens from Flint, Michigan, who noticed something seriously wrong with their drinking water. The tap water was brownish yellow and smelled like rotten eggs. Edwards specializes in fixing aging water systems in crumbling American cities. He sometimes describes his job in police terms, calling himself a crime scene investigator, or CSI, of plumbing. After conducting research in Flint, Edwards discovered that the tap water flowing into thousands of homes contained unsafe levels of lead. High levels of this heavy metal are toxic to the human body.

It did not take Edwards long to solve the mystery of Flint's contaminated water. The water was tainted by corrosion in the city's lead water pipes, which were more than a century old. As the Flint water crisis unfolded, Edwards participated in televised news conferences. His words were featured in dozens of news articles throughout the world. Edwards was instrumental in drawing attention to the problem. He set up a website to update the public on his scientific findings while encouraging citizens to hold government officials accountable.

In early 2016 Michigan governor Rick Snyder appointed Edwards to head a seventeen-member task force called the Flint Water Interagency Coordinating Committee to find a long-term solution to Flint's water crisis. Edwards was acclaimed by *Time* magazine, which placed him on a list of the one hundred most influential people of 2015. Two years later, Edwards was named Virginia Outstanding Scientist of 2017.

From Skyscrapers to Water Pipes

As an environmental engineer, Edwards uses chemical, biological, and other scientific principles to study how human activities impact the environment. But as environmental engineer and teacher Christine Cunningham explains, Edwards follows scientific processes common to all who work in the engineering field: "Engineers must identify the problem they are trying to solve, propose various solutions, test them out, gather data and use that all again. It's an iterative [repetitive] process. No matter what the exact field is, that goes across all engineering."[1]

There are few careers as versatile as engineering and few aspects of modern life that are untouched by engineers. Civil engineers create infrastructure, including sewers, dams, freeways, bridges, and skyscrapers. Aerospace engineers design the most advanced jet airplanes and spacecraft. Computer engineers, software engineers, and electrical engineers are responsible for the Internet, smartphones, and hundreds of devices connected to the World Wide Web. Industrial and mechanical engineers produce the latest innovations in robotics. Engineers who work in genetics and biomedicine are curing diseases and extending the human life span.

> "Engineers must identify the problem they are trying to solve, propose various solutions, test them out, gather data and use that all again. It's an iterative [repetitive] process. No matter what the exact field is, that goes across all engineering."[1]
>
> —Christine Cunningham, environmental engineer and teacher

Environmental engineers perform some of the most important work in modern society. They use chemistry, biology, and other sciences to mitigate the impact of human activities on the environment. Environmental engineers design systems, processes, and equipment to reduce the impact of air and water pollution created by factories. In places where industrial waste contaminates the environment, engineers design ways to mitigate the impact and clean up the toxins.

Some environmental engineers are concerned with cleaning up wastewater—sewage that is contaminated with detergents, personal care products, and human waste. Others work with public utilities to ensure a safe water supply. They design and monitor equipment that removes contaminants and develop systems to guarantee that tap water is pleasant tasting and safe to drink. When water is tainted, environmental engineers work to determine the cause.

While many environmental engineers work to maintain breathable air and clean water, others are developing cutting-edge technologies that will reduce the use of fossil fuels that contribute to climate change. Environmental engineers are working on systems to generate power from the energy of ocean waves. They are studying organic materials that can be used to create biological batteries, or biobatteries. Environmental engineers are harvesting biogas from rotting garbage in landfills and designing ultramodern buildings that use zero net energy.

A Critical Role

Although Edwards was lauded as a hero, the work of environmental engineers is largely unacknowledged by the general public. Most Americans never wonder where their water comes from, how their sewage is treated, why the air is not choked with smog, or where their garbage goes after the bin is emptied and left on the curb. But the systems that allow people to coexist with nature and live healthy, happy lives are central to those who make their careers as environmental engineers.

The United States is an industrial society with powerful mining, drilling, and manufacturing interests, and environmental engineers work every day to minimize the damage from waste and pollution. Although the research, inventions, and systems deployed for these important tasks often remain relatively unknown to the public, the environmental engineers behind them play a critical role in modern society.

CHAPTER 1

What Does an Environmental Engineer Do?

Environmental engineers are dedicated to protecting ecosystems and conserving natural resources. And they do so in many different ways. Some environmental engineers compile data to show how the construction of roads and buildings will impact the environment. Those who specialize as hydrologists provide input for government agencies looking to dredge rivers, maintain water quality in lakes and reservoirs, and prepare for flood emergencies. Still others focus on protecting endangered species. These environmental engineers interpret the complex natural laws that account for animal migration, nesting patterns, feeding zones, and critical habitats. The work involves filling out environmental impact statements required by government regulators, helping companies obtain building permits, and developing construction plans and building systems that preserve animal habitat.

Some of the most important work of environmental engineers concerns balancing the needs of industry, the environment, and public health. This is especially important when it comes to providing clean, pollution-free tap water for public consumption. Environmental engineers who work at water treatment plants operate computerized control systems and monitor water filtration equipment in a multistage process that removes everything from twigs and leaves to microorganisms that can transmit diseases such as cholera, typhoid fever, and dysentery. Environmental engineers read flow meters, gauges, and other recording instruments; collect and test water samples for chemical and bacterial content; and adjust plant equipment to ensure clean water output. The job also entails writing reports, compiling statistics on water quality, and keeping logs pertaining to maintenance and other tasks.

The flip side of producing clean drinking water is processing the wastewater that flows down drains, toilets, and sewers. Wastewater treatment plants often operate side by side with water treatment plants, and environmental engineers perform similar tasks at both types of facilities. Environmental engineer Kerry-Anne Taylor manages the Bennery Lake Water Supply Plant in Nova Scotia, Canada, which produces drinking water and treats wastewater. Taylor explains why her career is satisfying: "It's a feel-good job. I feel good about providing safe water for people. And, on the wastewater treatment side, I feel good about helping the environment. I always wanted a job like that."[2]

> "I feel good about providing safe water for people. And, on the wastewater treatment side, I feel good about helping the environment. I always wanted a job like that."[2]
>
> —Kerry-Anne Taylor, environmental engineer

Tackling Problems at High-Profile Resorts

In 2014 environmental engineers at Ohio University studied water systems, sewage treatment plants, and other infrastructure at numerous high-profile coastal resorts around the world. The engineers pored over statistics concerning rainfall, freshwater resources, water pollution problems, and solid waste produced by tourists.

The environmental engineers learned that 80 percent of the world's top tourist sites are built on ecologically sensitive ocean coastlines. And the environmental impact of tourism is causing lasting harm in some regions. Many resorts are built in areas with little rainfall and that have limited sources of freshwater. But hotel showers, swimming pools, restaurants, and golf courses use massive amounts of water.

Wastewater and garbage pose other problems at tourist resorts. During the busiest months, so much sewage and solid waste is produced that it overwhelms the carrying capacities of the local treatment plants and landfills. This means excessive sewage,

A hydrologist reads the weight of California's Sierra snowpack to help determine the state's water resources for the coming year. This is one of the jobs done by environmental engineers.

plastic, and other waste ends up polluting the very beaches and freshwater supplies that tourism depends on. Another pollution problem affects coral reefs, which provide extremely important habitat for numerous sea creatures. Environmentalists often encourage tourists to snorkel around coral reefs because the activity can educate visitors and help promote preservation. Ironically, however, the sunscreen worn by snorkelers contains chemicals that are toxic to coral reefs.

Promoting Sustainable Tourism

After finishing their extensive tourist resort study, Ohio University's environmental engineers proposed engineering solutions to promote sustainable coastal tourism. The engineers focused their expertise on increasing freshwater supplies, managing wastewater, and preserving coral reefs. The environmental engineers figured that the best way to increase water supplies was to harvest millions of gallons of rainwater that is wasted after storms. The rain cascades off buildings, parking lots, sidewalks, and roads; runs down gutters into storm drains; and funnels into the sea. In response to this problem, the environmental engineers created buildings designed to trap rainwater. Hotels were redesigned with rooftop pools surrounded by low concrete walls that collected rain as it fell. Attached downspouts transferred rainwater to concrete cisterns, or large storage tanks, located in the building's basement. The environmental engineers also created a system that cleaned the rainwater, making it drinkable by passing it through specially designed filters.

The environmental engineers who worked on wastewater problems created systems that allowed hotels to recycle the mix of soap and water called gray water. This water drains from sinks, showers, and washing machines and is usually flushed into sewer systems. One engineering approach involved constructing wetlands. The wetlands could be built on rooftops or next to buildings and planted with wetland plants that provide the cleansing functions of a marsh in nature. The soap and dirt in gray water is removed by wetland plants, bacteria, and other natural systems. The water recycled this way can be used to water plants, flush toilets, and fill washing machines.

Detecting and Cleaning Up Pollution

Like their counterparts working in popular tourist resorts, environmental engineers in urban areas also help solve problems. These engineers address industrial pollution, which poses a major threat to freshwater resources. Before modern environmental laws were enacted, companies that produced paint, pesticides, petroleum, and plastics released hazardous materials into the environment. Although environmental laws have curbed some of these contaminants, pollution continues to make its way into the environment through accidents or improperly functioning equipment. Many industrial toxins in freshwater, such as dioxin, polychlorinated biphenyl, lead, chromium, and benzene, are associated with cancer, reproductive problems, and learning disorders.

Environmental engineers design systems to clean up water and soil pollution, a process known as environmental remediation. They begin the process by visiting the polluted site and running tests to determine the types of toxins that are present and the extent of the contamination. In some areas pollution is caused by chemicals spilled on the topsoil, but in other places the pollution has seeped into surface waters or water below the surface, called groundwater. There are many different remediation techniques, and environmental engineers are constantly developing new technologies to deal with pollution.

When inspecting polluted sites, environmental engineers thoroughly map the area to determine its physical features, size, and the exact location of the pollution. After analyzing and mapping a site, environmental engineers decide on the most appropriate methods for remediation. They identify hazards that might harm cleanup workers and evaluate how the project will affect the nearby community and the overall environment of the area. For example, local streets might be negatively impacted by traffic, dust, and air pollution if dozens of dump trucks are used to remove contaminated soil.

Environmental engineers also must decide where the contaminated soil will be disposed of and how much it will cost. If the pollution is radioactive or extremely toxic, the soil must be placed in special containers and hauled to a secure storage facility. If the groundwater is contaminated, environmental engineers devise systems that can be used to pump the water out of the ground, treat it, and return it to its place of origin. Once cleanup begins, environmental engineers might operate or modify industrial equipment that is used for remediation. After the project is completed, the engineers inspect the site and ensure that it complies with local, state, and federal environmental laws.

Remediation is often carried out in places known as brownfields, which are abandoned commercial or industrial sites where the environment is contaminated by hazardous substances or pol-

The Envirobot Snake

In Switzerland, environmental engineers used their skills to develop a pollution-seeking robotic snake called the Envirobot. The 4-foot-long (1.2 m) device is made from segments that flex in a coordinated manner and allow the Envirobot to swim like a snake. The head contains the so-called brains—a camera, power supply, and computer that guide the mechanical snake. The segments that make up the body contain electrical and chemical sensors that measure acidity, alkalinity, salinity, and other qualities of concern in water. Segments with biological sensors contain living microorganisms that can be used to detect toxins such as insecticides.

Tiny electric motors drive the Envirobot through waterways. The motors are guided by information from the sensors in other segments that allow the robot to find a source of pollution. Environmental engineer Auke Ijspeert explains the many advantages to snake-like robots: "They can take measurements and send us data in real time—much faster than if we had measurement stations set up around the lake. And compared with conventional propeller-driven underwater robots, they are less likely to get stuck in algae or branches as they move around. What's more, they produce less of a wake, so they don't disperse pollutants as much."

Quoted in Devin Coldewey, "The Envirobot Robo-eel Slithers Along the Shore for Science," TechCrunch, June 25, 2017. https://techcrunch.com.

lution. According to the Environmental Protection Agency (EPA), there are more than 450,000 brownfields in the United States where chemical plants, steel mills, and other polluting businesses were once located. The sites, which can range in size from a corner lot to several thousand acres, are often located in urban areas. Some environmental engineers specialize in cleaning up brownfields so they can be redeveloped into shopping centers, business campuses, or parks.

In 2017 an abandoned gas station became the focus for environmental engineers in Chicopee, Massachusetts. The gas station, which dated back to the 1920s, was abandoned in 2004. The city, working with a $100,000 grant from the EPA, hired an environmental engineering firm to conduct a targeted brownfield assessment (TBA) meant to evaluate the pollution on the small parcel of land. The TBA showed the soil was polluted from decades of gasoline spills. Additionally, the site contained several underground tanks that had leaked for years. The contamination posed a risk to human health and the environment. A second EPA grant paid for environmental engineers to oversee removal of the tanks and pavement. The dirt was dug up, disposed of, and replaced with clean soil. After the work was completed, environmental engineers monitored the area to ensure the contaminants were gone. The city plans to build an electric car–charging station where the polluting gas station once stood. But environmental engineers in Chicopee will stay busy—the city has fifteen more brownfield sites that require remediation.

Focusing on Climate Change

While some environmental engineers focus on brownfield remediation and other problems at specific locations, others specialize in "big picture" concerns associated with climate change. Engineers examining climate change solutions are working to create systems that will mitigate the effects of carbon dioxide (CO_2), the greenhouse gas produced when fossil fuels are burned.

In 2017 engineers at Washington University in St. Louis established the Consortium for Clean Coal Utilization to invent new ways to reduce the CO_2 emitted by coal-burning power plants in India and China, the two countries with the world's fastest-growing economies. China produces 70 percent of its electricity with coal and is responsible for almost 30 percent of the world's greenhouse gas emissions.

Twenty environmental engineers at the Washington University facility are collaborating with seventeen engineers in China and India to develop technology that will reduce CO_2 emissions at coal power plants. The engineers are designing complex systems that burn coal at much higher temperatures and under greater pressure. These designs use less coal than traditional power plants and will allow plants to produce electricity much more efficiently. Environmental engineering professor Richard Axelbaum explains the importance of the work: "By collaborating with [engineers] in these countries, we are able to work together to develop technologies that will allow them to still use this resource, but in a way that has minimal impact on the environment, both locally and globally."[3]

Utilizing Existing Technology

Renewable energy projects are another focus for environmental engineers who want to address climate change issues. One of the greatest challenges concerns harnessing the energy found in the endless crashing of ocean waves on a beach. Wave energy is produced by the movement of the ocean and the changing heights and speed of the swells. A single 4-foot-tall (1.2 m) wave crashing on 1 mile (1.6 km) of coastline contains energy equal to around twenty-six average wind turbines. However, harvesting that energy remains an elusive goal; the ocean environment is hostile and unpredictable.

Environmental engineer Craig Jones is hoping his work will help his colleagues design and build wave energy projects by precisely measuring the movements of waves. Backed by a grant from the Department of Energy, Jones designed a low-cost solar-powered buoy called Spotter. The buoy provides real-time wave-by-wave information that is delivered to a smartphone app. Spotter is a major improvement over the buoys currently in use, which were developed during the 1980s and cost as much as $50,000. Due to the expense of these buoys, many organizations that want to collect good wave data cannot afford to do so. Spotter, however, costs less than $5,000 and provides much greater detail and accuracy. Jones describes the inspiration for Spotter: "In doing more personal research into wave measurement, we realized that most of the technology needed to make highly accurate wave measurements is readily available, including in the smart phones in our own pockets. . . . Utilization of

"In doing more personal research into wave measurement, we realized that most of the technology needed to make highly accurate wave measurements is readily available, including in the smart phones in our own pockets."[4]

—Craig Jones, environmental engineer

existing tools [can] lead to techniques that can address the problems we have."[4]

In addition to developing Spotter, Jones has developed engineering and science programs for government agencies and private companies. He has also testified on environmental issues in federal court and before public utilities commissions that oversee water and electric utilities. Jones's work incorporates math, science, biology, computer technology, and more. His career achievements provide a great example of how environmental engineers can be involved in many important issues. From providing clean water to tackling climate change, environmental engineers perform critical work that balances the needs of modern society with the essentials of preserving sensitive ecosystems.

CHAPTER 2

How Do You Become an Environmental Engineer?

When environmental engineer and teacher Christine Cunningham was growing up in Boston during the 1990s she often spent time at home with her mother conducting science experiments. These experiments taught Cunningham that science could be very interesting. But according to Cunningham, "What I was experiencing in school wasn't the same kind of experience I was having at home."[5] Her school science experiments were boring and varied little from the type of experiments kids had been conducting for decades.

This realization later led Cunningham to develop the Engineering Is Elementary curriculum for Boston's Museum of Science. The program is aimed at elementary and middle school kids who wish to pursue a career in engineering. Cunningham explains the rationale behind Engineering Is Elementary: "The engineering design process can help us solve engineering problems, but it can also help solve myriad other problems. So if we can equip our students with a mindset and a set of habits of mind that allow them to encounter problems they've never seen before, I think we equip them for the future in better ways than traditional science can."[6] Cunningham's advice about developing a problem-solving mindset can apply to anyone who wishes to pursue a career as an environmental engineer.

Study Math in High School

Mathematics is central to solving engineering problems. As engineer Jack Nixon explains, "Engineers take the theories of the mathematicians and put them to practical use."[7] Prospective environmental engineers need to become proficient in math while still in high school. Students should study algebra, geometry, trigonometry, differential equations, statistics, and calculus. Each math topic has a unique purpose in the field of environmental engineering. For example, trigonometry is the science of measuring triangles. Environmental engineers use a type of math called plane trigonometry to determine the size of a parcel of land that has an irregular shape. Spherical trigonometry might be used by an environmental engineer designing a mechanical hand for a robot.

> "Engineers take the theories of the mathematicians and put them to practical use."[7]
>
> —Jack Nixon, engineer

Statistics is another extremely important type of math used by environmental engineers who work with wastewater, hazardous materials remediation, and air pollution problems. Environmental engineers study statistics to determine how much rain historically falls in a region, how strong the winds are, or how much of a chemical is present in a body of water. Environmental scientist Fred Vreeman explains the importance of other branches of mathematics: "[Students] should know . . . calculus, differential equations, and linear algebra. Without this you cannot understand the [origins] of the equations used to describe mechanical and physical properties of the environment."[8] Vreeman says high school students who wish to pursue careers as environmental engineers should also study physics during their sophomore and junior years of high school.

Obtain a Bachelor's Degree

All environmental engineers hold a bachelor's degree in engineering, environmental engineering, or a related field such as civil or chemical engineering. Students enrolling in an environmental engineering degree program should choose one that is certified by the Accreditation Board for Engineering and Technology (ABET). This organization provides assurance that the program meets the quality standards of the engineering profession.

Environmental engineering students can expect to study basic engineering priciples, ecosystem processes, organic pollutants, alternative energy technologies, air quality control systems, water and wastewater treatment, and principles of sustainability. Students pursuing an environmental engineering degree usually participate in specific programs within their engineering departments. These programs include water resources engineering, municipal water/wastewater engineering, industrial water/wastewater engineering, air pollution engineering, and hazardous waste remediation engineering. Those who concentrate on solid waste engineering learn the technical details of landfills, trash incineration, and related issues. Some environmental engineering programs focus on coastal and ocean engineering, which emphasizes coastal climate change topics such as rises in sea levels, coastal storms, marine renewable energy, marine ecology, and natural coastal hazards, including tsunamis and hurricanes.

Students studying for engineering degrees need a basic understanding of chemistry and biology. They take biology and chemistry during their freshman year. Sophomore year courses focus on organic chemistry. Environmental engineering students also need to understand soil classification, a study that separates soil into classes or groups that have similar engineering properties. The basics of soil classification, such as permeability, stiffness, and strength, are taught in geology courses. Geology also covers concepts of geotechnical engineering, a branch of engineering that focuses on the behavior of soil, rocks, and other subsurface materials.

Hydrology focuses on many environmental engineering concepts, such as water supplies, storm sewer designs, irrigation system designs, stream restoration, and drought mitigation. Hydrology also covers topics such as the quality, movement, storage, and distribution of water and the way water interacts with environmental and human activities. Hydrogeology is the area of geology that applies to underground water sources, or groundwater. Both hydrology and hydrogeology are mandatory subjects for prospective environmental engineers. Engineering students study the physical processes that affect water quality, including precipitation, evaporation, filtration, and stream flow. They learn mathematical descriptions of these processes as well as statistical methods associated with hydrological systems.

Students studying environmental engineering can take other relevant courses to develop specific skills. For example, mechanical engineering teaches students about machinery and mechanical systems, some of which are used by environmental engineers to pump water, treat wastewater, process garbage, and perform other tasks. Courses in environmental chemistry, sustainable chemistry, and environmental chemical engineering provide an understanding of the way chemicals, both good and bad, affect human health and the environment. Environmental technology courses are designed to teach students how to design and build devices that monitor or control pollution or produce energy from renewable resources.

A Graduate Degree in Environmental Engineering

Engineering is known as a very difficult major, and some students are reluctant to obtain a graduate degree after they have completed their undergraduate courses. However, students who attend graduate school will earn more and have more independence. A master's degree in environmental engineering usually takes one to three years, and a doctorate requires a five- to six-year commitment.

Graduate programs are designed to give pupils advanced knowledge about natural and built environments. Course work may include air quality, water chemistry, fluid mechanics, microbiology, and environmental law and policy. Working closely with professors, students conduct research and develop skills needed to design, plan, and implement environmental projects involving water treatment, emission controls, solid waste disposal remedies, or other topics geared to a student's area of interest.

Those who wish to teach at the university level or conduct environmental research need to obtain a doctorate. This process requires students to be accepted into a program, complete course work, and write a lengthy research-based essay called a dissertation. Before writing the doctoral essay, the candidate creates a

Ranking Engineering Graduate Schools

Every year the magazine *U.S. News & World Report* produces a list of the best colleges and grad schools. According to the magazine's 2017 ranking, the top graduate programs for environmental engineers can be found at the University of California–Berkeley (UCB); the University of Illinois at Urbana-Champaign; Stanford University; and the University of Michigan. Full-time in-state tuition at UCB was $11,220, and out-of-state students could expect to pay $26,322.

Berkeley students typically complete their master's degree in two years, but some opt for the accelerated Berkeley Engineering Professional Master's Program, which allows students to graduate in one year. All graduate students must also complete two minors. The College of Engineering has forty research centers where graduate students can work on their dissertations.

Stanford is considerably more expensive than most universities; in 2017 students paid $50,424 per year. The school has sixty-five research centers and labs where students can complete their projects. Stanford is in the heart of California's Silicon Valley, and many local tech companies offer internships to grad students.

dissertation proposal, which describes an original, doctoral-level research project. The dissertation proposal must be approved by a dissertation committee made up of four or five professors selected by the student. Members of the dissertation committee guide and encourage a doctoral candidate during the dissertation-writing process.

Upon completion, the doctoral candidate presents what is called a dissertation defense. The student presents, explains, and defends the ideas in the dissertation. Committee members may ask questions and discuss points of interest among themselves. Candidates will often be asked to point out the weaknesses in their project. After the defense, the candidate leaves the room and the committee deliberates before voting whether to pass the dissertation. The desired outcome is when the candidate comes back into the room and hears the statement "Congratulations, Dr. _____". This means the candidate has earned a doctoral degree and can now be referred to as *Doctor*.

Internships, Co-ops, and Research Teams

Most students in environmental engineering programs gain hands-on experience with internships while still in college. Internships give students an opportunity to work in a professional environment, obtain good references, and develop a network of like-minded professionals. All this gives students a competitive advantage when job hunting after graduation.

An Internet search of the phrase *environmental engineer internships* reveals numerous opportunities in every state. Engineer Frank Wouters recommends calling environmental engineering firms—rather than e-mailing them—to ask if they offer internships. If a firm does not have an internship program, someone at the organization might be able to recommend a company that does. If an internship is available, the candidate should be prepared to immediately send a cover letter and résumé. Wouters offers this advice: "Don't hesitate to ask your teachers for help in creating a good résumé and introduction [letter]. These things are pretty important . . . later in life, so they are crucial to master."[9]

> "Don't hesitate to ask your teachers for help in creating a good résumé and introduction [letter]. These things are pretty important . . . later in life, so they are crucial to master."[9]
>
> —Frank Wouters, engineer

Students who are in their sophomore year can apply for cooperative education programs (co-ops) at private environmental engineering companies or at a government agency like the EPA. Students in co-ops stop taking classes to work full-time. The positions typically pay from fifteen to twenty dollars an hour and last anywhere from three to twelve months. Students receive an academic credit and a letter grade for their paid work experience.

Students might also be able to sign up with a university research team to work with a professor on an environmental engineering research project. Those who gain experience analyzing and testing data will find that their skills are in demand in the workplace.

Licensing

Environmental engineers seeking an entry-level position do not need any type of license. However, those who become licensed professional engineers (PEs) can obtain higher salaries and advanced positions of leadership. A PE license allows the holder to oversee the work of other engineers, give final approval to projects, and provide services directly to individual clients (as opposed to working for a company or engineering firm).

Those who wish to become licensed PEs need a degree from an ABET-accredited engineering program and must pass two exams. Recent graduates who have earned their bachelor's degree in environmental engineering can take the computer-based Fundamentals of Engineering exam, which includes 110 questions that must be answered within six hours. Those who pass the exam are called engineers in training or engineer interns. After at least four years of relevant work experience, candidates take a second exam, called the Principles and Practice of Engineering. The exam contains 80 multiple-choice questions and is administered over the course of eight hours.

Students Changing Lives

The services provided by environmental engineers are needed all over the world. Some who are working toward obtaining their bachelor's or master's degrees begin their careers by joining the organization Engineers Without Borders, which operates chapters on many college campuses. In 2017 students working for the organization were providing solar power to a refugee camp in Bhutan, implementing water and sanitation systems in Nicaragua, and helping water and power utilities in flood-ravaged Houston test and repair their systems. Although it takes hard work and dedication to become an environmental engineer, students who pursue this career path develop valuable skills that can change lives and make the world a safer, cleaner, better place to live.

CHAPTER 3

What Skills and Personal Qualities Matter Most— and Why?

The word *engineer* is derived from the same Latin root as *ingenuity*. Engineers rely on ingenuity—that is, imagination and creativity—to observe, analyze, and devise solutions to highly technical environmental problems. As civil engineer G. Wayne Clough asserts, "Engineering is a profoundly creative process." However, Clough also points out that the creativity of environmental engineers is often restricted by real-world limitations: "A most elegant description is that engineering is about [creative] design under constraint. . . . A successful design, in the sense that it leads . . . to an improvement in our quality of life, must work within the constraints provided by technical, economic, business, political, social, and ethical issues."[10]

Environmental engineers must develop a number of skills and talents to work creatively within the limitations of the job. The essential skills can be divided into three broad categories: technical, operational, and awareness skills. Environmental engineers rely on technical skills, based on education and experience, to analyze and understand problems. They use operational skills to carry out processes and procedures necessary to complete tasks. And environmental engineers utilize awareness skills, which help them consider the impact their engineering solutions will have on the economy, the environment, and society.

Technical Skills

At the most basic level, the job of an environmental engineer is to solve logistical problems using science, technology, engineering, and math. Professionals in the field of environmental engineering base their findings on scientific rules and methods. They rely on mathematics to invent or adapt systems, components, and processes for engineering solutions. Environmental engineers need to be familiar with other branches of technology, including information and communications technology, biotechnology (the use of biological processes to solve technical problems), and nanotechnology (the manipulation of individual atoms and molecules).

> "Engineering is a profoundly creative process."[10]
>
> —G. Wayne Clough, civil engineer

Environmental engineers use their technical skills to design and conduct experiments while searching for new ways to address problems. They rely on strong analytical skills to identify the strengths and weaknesses of experiments. This skill allows them to use impartial analysis to evaluate the technical solutions that result from experimentation, which must work outside the lab as practical applications in real-world conditions. A talent for logic and reasoning helps environmental engineers find solutions that function within the framework of budgets, building schedules, and public concerns about sustainability and the environment. Combining technical expertise with analytical skills is not always easy, as engineering recruiter and career coach Nader Mowlaee explains: "Knowledge is power, but it is not always what you know, it's how you use it. . . . Not everyone uses that knowledge in the same way. This is primarily because it's a special skill to organize our thoughts and implement them . . . during the planning and execution process of every project."[11]

Operational Skills

The practical aspects of planning and implementing successful projects oblige environmental engineers to develop operational skills. These capabilities are needed to transform a blueprint or experiment into a finished product. Many operational abilities are referred to as soft skills, which generally refer to the capacity to work well with others. A blogger known as 3DX explains, "Nobody completes an engineering project by themselves: there is a vast team working on various parts of the project."[12] This means environmental engineers must work well with groups, including members from culturally diverse research teams, global corporations, and experts from other scientific disciplines.

Team players need excellent communication skills to translate the technical language of engineering into plain English for multiple stakeholders in a project, which might include government regulators, business customers, environmentalists, and the general public. According to Mowlaee, environmental engineers must be able to simplify the extreme complexity of a project: "A great engineer will be able to explain a task, project or set of goals in simple terms so that it can be understood smoothly. This is one of the personality traits that are tough to have as the work we do becomes more complicated."[13]

The desire to continue to learn throughout a career is another operational skill used by environmental engineers. Continual learning is necessary because technology changes rapidly and environmental engineers are facing new challenges every day. As Stanford engineering professor James Plummer explains, "Lifelong learning is essential. The half-life of engineering knowledge is three to five years."[14] What Plummer means is that half of everything an environmental engineer knows today will be obsolete in a few years. This means environmental engineers need to stay informed about changes and developments in sustainable water sources, solid waste management, and water and air pollution monitoring. And in the future that half-life might be even shorter, requiring environmental engineers to update their expertise even more often.

As the population grows, new solutions will be needed to avoid ecological damage while growing more food, constructing

> "Lifelong learning is essential. The half-life of engineering knowledge is three to five years."[14]
>
> —James Plummer, engineering professor

One of the skills required of environmental engineers is the ability to transform a blueprint or other hard data into a report or product that can be used by other team members who are all working on the same project.

new housing, and manufacturing a greater number of cars and consumer goods. Coping with climate change will present the biggest challenge, and only those who are dedicated to lifelong learning will be equipped to make the most out of developments in environmental engineering.

An Awareness of Social Issues

Environmental engineers do not operate in a vacuum separate from society. They need to develop awareness skills to consider the social, cultural, and political impacts of a project. As a National Academy of Engineering report explains, "Consideration of social issues is central to engineering. . . . [Attention to] multilingual

Ingenuity and Future Challenges

G. Wayne Clough, a leader in engineering education and research, describes the importance of ingenuity for engineers:

Using science and practical ingenuity, engineers identify problems and find solutions. This will continue to be a mainstay of engineering. But as technology continues to increase in complexity and the world becomes ever more dependent on technology, the magnitude, scope, and impact of the challenges society will face in the future are likely to change. For example, issues related to climate change, the environment, and the intersections between technology and social/public policies are becoming increasingly important. . . . The need for practical solutions will be at or near critical stage, and engineers, and their ingenuity, will become ever more important.

Creativity (invention, innovation, thinking outside the box, art) is an indispensable quality for engineering, and given the growing scope of the challenges ahead and the complexity and diversity of the technologies of the 21st century, creativity will grow in importance.

G. Wayne Clough et al., "The Engineer of 2020," National Academy of Engineering, 2017. www.nap.edu.

influences and cultural diversity, moral/religious repercussions, global/international impacts, national security, and cost-benefit constraints will continue to drive engineering practice."[15]

Those who are successful as lead engineers on a project have highly developed awareness skills. Team leaders provide clear guidance and direction to other members and are willing to listen to others, take advice, and provide support. They know when to step in to help struggling coworkers, and they know when to back off if their advice is not needed. Leaders need to understand how to utilize the strengths of others and when to discipline workers who need to be reined in.

Leaders set realistic goals; they do not create schedules or develop plans that are too ambitious. Goals can be challenging, but they also must be achievable or else the project might be of poor quality or never get finished. Setting realistic goals is part of a leader's role in setting a good example for others. Additionally, leaders must have high ethical standards and a strong sense of professionalism. Leaders use resources in a wise and prudent manner and keep everyone informed about a project's progress and problems. And leadership requires trust and honesty, as Mowlaee explains: "You should be honest even if the situation will not favor you, even if it is painful to deal with and even if it contradicts the needs, desires, beliefs, and intentions of the organization. . . . Projects tend to fail with dishonesty as the problems that arise may not be addressed properly."[16]

Awareness skills encompass concepts that cannot be learned from a book or in a classroom. Successful environmental engineers need to be open-minded and willing to change plans and adapt to new conditions when unforeseen problems arise. This mindset requires environmental engineers to see the big picture and concentrate on the outcome while overlooking small problems and immediate concerns. This type of focus helps environmental engineers plan for any conceivable problems that might arise. By thinking ahead, environmental engineers are not caught off guard. They have contingency procedures in place when the unexpected happens. A focus on the big picture also allows professionals to take advantage of new opportunities, such as the introduction of a new technology or a new way of completing a project with more efficiency or at a lower cost.

"Essential Skills in Common"

Being an environmental engineer is not easy, and the job comes with great responsibilities. Well-honed technical and operational talents and a heightened awareness make it easier for an environmental engineer to find success and satisfaction. But it is not necessary for a single individual to possess every talent and skill, as blogger 3DX writes: "The 'top' [environmental] engineers all have different strengths and weaknesses that they bring to their teams and projects. However, they have some essential skills in common which allow them to work on the biggest engineering projects all over the world."[17]

While students might be intimidated when contemplating the abilities and personality traits of top environmental engineers, these attributes are developed and refined over time. Honing the skills for success only requires a prospective environmental engineer to be motivated by a desire for self-improvement. In the coming years, the environmental engineering community will face unprecedented and unpredictable problems. Those who are ingenious and ethical global citizens, with strong analytical, professional, and leadership skills, will be in the best position to advance their careers while meeting the challenges of the future.

CHAPTER 4

What Is It Like to Work as an Environmental Engineer?

As the job title of environmental engineer suggests, those involved in this line of work spend their time in many different environments. Environmental engineers conduct fieldwork in the natural world, in urban areas, along riverbanks and lakeshores, and next to highways and pipelines. They visit factories, water pumping stations, sewage treatment plants, and construction sites. When they are not out in the field, environmental engineers work on computers in offices, studying statistics, conducting research, and designing tools and systems. Lab work entails conducting experiments and testing samples of water, chemicals, and other substances. Environmental engineers are also likely to attend seminars where they give presentations and interact with other professionals in the field.

Four out of five environmental engineers work full-time. But about 20 percent work more than forty hours a week when they are required to monitor a project's progress and ensure that various deadlines are met.

Conducting Environmental Fieldwork

Ari Cheremeteff is an environmental engineer who spends her days outdoors working to minimize the impact of chemical pollution on the urban environment of Rochester, New York. Cheremeteff is employed by Lu Engineers, a civil and environmental engineering firm. Rochester has many brownfields that once held abandoned gas stations, factories, and other businesses. When the companies closed, they left behind a variety of highly toxic compounds that pose a danger to public health. Leaders in Rochester want to revitalize the city's economy by developing these brownfields.

One aspect of the job of an environmental engineer is fieldwork. This might involve visits to factories or pumping stations or other facilities to monitor water quality.

Cheremeteff specializes in environmental remediation, the process of removing pollution and other contaminants from the soil and groundwater. Cheremeteff comments on the focus of her job: "I want to see Rochester use a lot of the spaces that are unused because of environmental issues. [I want] to bring function to the city . . . while keeping humans from being exposed to toxins."[18]

When Cheremeteff visits brownfields, she takes soil and water samples, conducts ecological surveys, and maps the various features of the land. After developing remediation plans, she oversees contractors who inject what is called bioremediation material into the soil of contaminated sites. The material contains bacteria that eat petroleum and other toxins. Cheremeteff uses computers, global positioning system (GPS) programs, and old maps and blueprints to chart out the exact distance between each bacteria injection spot to ensure the best results. After the material is injected into the soil, she returns to the site and conducts tests to make sure the remediation was effective. If more needs to be done, Cheremeteff works with the remediation contractors to augment previous efforts. As Cheremeteff explains, "Each site is very different, so finding the right plan or approach takes a lot of research and collaboration with [others on my team]. It's a fun challenge. That's part of the allure for me."[19]

Conducting inspections is a big part of an environmental engineer's job. An environmental engineer might specialize in inspecting wastewater treatment plants, sewage systems, air pollution abatement equipment in factories, or landfill designs. When a highway is built, environmental engineers are called in to conduct inspections of the work to ensure the road is not going to disturb a protected wetland or other sensitive ecosystem. An environmental engineer working as an inspector might return to the same site day after day to monitor the progress of a project.

Environmental engineer Nicole Zaidel lives in Wisconsin, where her job entails inspecting the energy systems employed by farmers. As an engineering adviser for a statewide program called Focus on Energy, Zaidel advises farmers about the financial incentives available for energy-efficiency projects. Zaidel provides technical assistance to farmers and contractors who retrofit their farms to install more efficient lighting and other electrical equipment. Once the systems are installed, Zaidel fills out the required approval forms to certify that the equipment is installed and functioning and submits forms that ensure her clients receive their rebates and other funds from the project.

No Two Days Are Alike

Although fieldwork is part of the job, environmental engineers generally spend around 80 percent of their time in an office. They conduct face-to-face meetings with clients, technical experts, contractors, city environmental officials, and others. Rachel Romero specializes in energy issues as an engineer for the National Renewable Energy Laboratory, working to make government buildings more energy efficient. Romero describes the balance between working in the field and in the office:

> I often meet in person with industry experts who make buildings more energy efficient. I use what I learn from

them as I walk through different kinds of buildings, finding ways to make them use less energy. I email and talk with people at the Department of Homeland Security to help them with their energy management program. I write about new ways to convey the message of how important energy efficiency is to my clients, who mostly work in different federal agencies.[20]

Much of the office work for an environmental engineer involves what is commonly referred to as paperwork, although it is completed using a computer. Those who work in this profession spend hours reviewing permits for environmental engineering projects to ensure the tasks comply with the dizzying array of regulations issued by local, state, and federal agencies. The environmental engineers review reports submitted by workers and government inspectors in the field. Sometimes this type of work can provide a steady job for decades, as an environmental engineer known online as InWyo explains: "The beauty of environmental engineering . . . [is that] sites take a really long time to clean up, and . . . require 30 years of monitoring, reporting and statistics after the site is closed."[21] However, as InWyo says, the work is not particularly exciting. He often compiles new statistics on landfills that have been closed for twenty-five years or more. He says adding one more data point to statistics spanning many decades can seem like a futile task.

Perhaps the most interesting aspect of office work involves design. Environmental engineers use computers to design pipelines, pumps, water treatment systems, and other infrastructure. They work with modeling software such as MATLAB and Microworlds to build digital models that allow them to understand how a device or structure will function in the real world. Three-dimensional (3-D) programs like AutoCAD are used to build models for 3-D environments. Environmental engineer Rajan Jha, who specializes in wastewater consulting, sums up his duties:

No two days are ever alike. . . . Some days I'm in the office, making a presentation to a client or working on the computer. I use all kinds of software to make challenging

"Engineer Thinking"

Anne Dare has a doctorate in environmental engineering and works for the US Agency for International Development. As Dare explains, her job has many unique aspects that go far beyond those of a typical engineer:

> One part of my job involves traveling to the Middle East to support scientists and engineers in conducting research and exploring ways we can encourage sustainable development and build peace in the region. Oftentimes, part of my day is also spent working with my colleagues in Washington, DC, on ways scientists and engineers can improve how they communicate complex, scientific information with one another, policymakers, and the public. . . .
>
> In Washington, DC, I have the opportunity to learn from an incredible range of people, from top academics to elected leaders and foreign diplomats. Many of my colleagues have degrees in international studies and foreign affairs and form a highly diverse, interdisciplinary team. After years in the field of engineering, I now work at the intersection of international development and policy and bring a science, technology, and evidence-driven approach to the table. I like that I get to insert "engineer thinking" into a non-engineering space.

Quoted in DiscoverE, "What Engineers Do," 2017. www.discovere.org.

design calculations, which are used to plan the construction of buildings, water distribution systems, and other projects. On other days I'm in the field, investigating pipe drains or building projects. Some of my most memorable work experiences have happened while I'm out in the field. I also travel to conferences where I showcase my work and learn from colleagues.[22]

In addition to the technical work, environmental engineers often perform managerial tasks. They assist in budgeting matters, produce business forecasts for their employers, and carry out general administrative duties.

Matters of Company Size

The workdays of environmental engineers vary depending on the size of the company where they are employed. Small firms, which typically employ fewer than one hundred people, are generally friendlier places to work. Workers know one another, and employees can usually arrange for quick meetings with the boss. Assignments are broader at small companies; an environmental engineer might take on every aspect of a project from initial planning to completing the job. And employees at small firms are often encouraged to take on assignments outside their zone of technical expertise. For example, an environmental engineer might be asked to perform the work of an electrical, civil, or computer engineer. The work atmosphere is also faster paced, as decisions are often made quickly and carried out rapidly.

Some environmental engineers thrive in small firms, but there are disadvantages. Small companies have fewer clients and can quickly go out of business if their client base shrinks. This means that engineers who work for small firms must spend time analyzing the financial health of the company. Engineering career consultant John A. Hoschette describes other challenges of working for a small company:

> Working for a small company presents special challenges. In a small company there are usually very limited resources to call upon. . . . To be successful at your assignments, you must develop a network outside the company; a network of people and other companies you can quickly call upon for help and guidance when you are faced with a problem you cannot solve yourself. In addition, you must be able to work independently and with little supervision or guidance.[23]

Working at a large firm, which might employ several thousand people, presents different challenges for environmental engineers. Those who work for large engineering corporations are often members of big teams and may feel invisible or anonymous. Engineers are often assigned single small tasks that are focused and narrow. However, large companies offer greater job security and benefits. Employees can draw on a profusion of technical resources and experts when working on assignments.

Job Satisfaction

Whatever the size of the company, environmental engineers work in a variety of economic sectors. According to the Bureau of Labor Statistics, 55,100 people were employed as environmental engineers in 2014, the most recent year for which statistics are available. Approximately 28 percent of those engineers worked in civil, environmental, or related engineering services firms. Twenty percent were employed by scientific and technical consulting services, and 21 percent worked for state or local governments. The federal government employed around 6 percent of the environmental engineering workforce.

Wherever they work, most environmental engineers are satisfied with their job. According to a survey by the *U.S. News & World Report*, the job of environmental engineer ranks number one in the category of best engineering jobs, ahead of mechanical engineer, civil engineer, and biomedical engineer. The ranking is based on many factors, including salary, stress level, and work-life balance. And as Jha explains, environmental engineering can provide personal fulfillment: "Becoming [an environmental] engineer has given me exactly the kind of lifestyle I've dreamed of. It is so satisfying to work with my team and finish a daunting task for a client. Meeting with clients, building design simulations, and presenting my work all over the world has shaped me to become what I call 'A Passionate Humane Engineer.'"[24]

"Working for a small company presents special challenges. In a small company there are usually very limited resources to call upon. . . . You must be able to work independently and with little supervision or guidance."[23]

—John A. Hoschette, engineering career consultant

Advancement and Other Job Opportunities

In 2016 the median pay for an environmental engineer was $84,890, according to the Bureau of Labor Statistics. The median salary is the one at which half the environmental engineers earn more and half earn less. The lowest-paid environmental engineers earned $50,000 or less, and the highest-paid ones earned more than $130,000. There are several factors that contribute to the difference between the highest and lowest wage earners. For example, the median wage for environmental engineers in southern states like Alabama and South Carolina was around $65,000, but those in California, Alaska, and other western states were earning over $95,000. Environmental engineers working for the federal government could earn over $102,000 annually, and those who worked for state governments brought in $74,700.

Median pay statistics are helpful, but they do not tell the entire story. Environmental engineering is a dynamic profession that offers many opportunities for advancement. However, those who achieve the highest pay levels are often those who write out detailed career plans in the early phases of their career. These environmental engineers assess what is most important to them and create a blueprint that will allow them to achieve their goals as their careers develop.

The Environmental Engineer Career Ladder

When most environmental engineers finish college, they go to work as junior engineers at an established engineering company. In this entry-level position, they are expected to be good team players who follow orders and take direction from engineers with more experience. Junior environmental engineers learn about teamwork by consulting with engineers of different disciplines and by understanding company policies and procedures. Although they are done with school, junior engineers are expected to continue developing their knowledge base and technical skills. And they must prove themselves to supervisors by performing their assignments successfully and finishing on schedule. These actions help them land more challenging assignments.

After three to five years on the job, junior environmental engineers usually advance to the next level. While they continue to focus on their technical specialties, environmental engineers at this stage often become team leaders for small groups. They share their vision of the project for the team and explain the roles and responsibilities of each team member. As leaders, they inspire others to support team efforts and accomplish group goals. Those who are successful in leading small teams might progress to the role of project leader. This person is responsible for guiding the actions of a number of small teams working on the same project. Those who succeed in this role advance their careers as

Environmental engineers who are looking for advancement opportunities might become lead engineers. The lead engineer oversees large projects and offers direction and guidance to other team members.

they prove their leadership abilities with their work. Another way for a project leader to advance is to enter a project into one of the engineering competitions held by professional organizations. Winners of these competitions are honored by their colleagues and are often rewarded with raises and promotions.

Environmental engineers who have been on the job five to ten years often act as mentors, counseling those with less experience, called protégés. Good mentors enhance the careers of protégés by providing technical and business advice. Workplace mentors help protégés demonstrate their skills by steering them toward challenging assignments. Mentors explain company policies, traditions, and values, share expertise, help protégés deal with setbacks and problems, and provide career coaching. And even those with experience as mentors continue to work with the mentors who guided them when they were new on the job, as environmental engineer Tasha Kamegai-Karadi explains: "I enjoy teaching junior engineers new technical skills and how to be leaders in the field—and I appreciate learning from my own mentor, who gives me great career advice."[25]

"I enjoy teaching junior engineers new technical skills and how to be leaders in the field—and I appreciate learning from my own mentor, who gives me great career advice."[25]

—Tasha Kamegai-Karadi, environmental engineer

After around ten years on the job, environmental engineers can advance to the role of lead engineer, directing the activities of several large teams. Lead engineers are called upon to meet the technical objectives of customers and oversee all aspects of a project's design, testing, building, and production. Environmental engineers who advance to this level are often regarded as industry experts. They might hold several patents for devices or systems they have invented. (A patent is a legal document that provides the holder the right to collect money from others who use the invention.)

Lead engineers are required to ensure that a project is completed on schedule and within budget. Good management and leadership skills allow an environmental engineer to organize teams, plan projects, set company objectives, work with customers, and solve

The Mentoring Process

The dictionary defines *mentor* as a wise and trusted counselor or teacher. John A. Hoschette, an engineering career consultant, describes the value of mentors for engineers:

> Sponsorship from a mentor is essential to getting the challenging assignments that provide you with the opportunity to perform and clearly demonstrate you are ready to [advance your career]. A good mentor is usually in a position to defend your abilities should they come into question by the management. He or she is the person who interacts with management to vouch for your suitability to handle difficult assignments. Your mentor is there recommending you for the assignment, clearly identifying you as the best candidate to successfully complete it. It is this type of sponsorship that will make you stand out from the crowd. . . .
>
> By developing a good relationship with a powerful mentor you assimilate power just by being associated with them, you send signals to other people in the organization that you are a member of a power team. You acquire some of your mentor's influence and will have resources behind you.

John A. Hoschette, *The Engineer's Career Guide*. Hoboken, NJ: John Wiley & Sons, 2010, p. 89.

problems. At this career level, environmental engineers might also hire and fire employees and offer raises and promotions.

Two Options

At some point in their careers, typically after ten to twenty years, environmental engineers generally pursue one of two options. They can either continue to work as technical staff engineers or they can move into management. Those who remain in the technical realm are responsible for overseeing major projects and creating successful products for their company. They publish technical

Excellence in Environmental Engineering

Every year the American Academy of Environmental Engineers and Scientists (AAEES) awards prizes for environmental engineering design, planning, research, sustainability, and operations management. The competition is meant to identify and reward the best environmental engineers.

Environmental engineer Chris Berch can attest to the fact that those who win the AAEES competition will see their careers advance. In 2015 Berch led a team that added a renewable power system to the water recycling plant owned by the Inland Empire Utilities Agency (IEUA) in Chino, California. The plant, which provides freshwater to around 875,000 people, runs on electricity generated by solar panels. However, solar energy is not available at night. Berch solved the problem by designing a battery storage system that is charged by the solar panels and runs the water recycling facility at night.

After winning the AAEES grand prize for environmental sustainability in 2017, Berch was promoted to executive manager of engineering by the IEUA. Berch commented on his promotion: "I have been part of a team that has implemented some of the most recognized and innovative environmental engineering projects . . . in the United States. I am excited about . . . [leading] the next phase of this talented and progressive agency."

Quoted in Inland Empire Utilities Agency, "The Inland Empire Utilities Agency Promotes Chris Berch to Executive Manager of Engineering/Assistant General Manager," press release, February 19, 2017. www.ieua.org.

papers and sometimes return to academia for advanced training and degrees. Technical staff engineers work with technical experts in other fields and those who are employed by their customers.

Environmental engineers who move into management need to draw on another set of skills. In this role, the engineers focus their talents on the overall financial success of their company. They oversee finances, banking, personnel, marketing, customer relations, and profit and loss. Some engineers return to school to obtain a master of business administration degree. Engineering career consultant John A. Hoschette describes the work of an environmental engineer who has reached this career level:

Engineering careers generally peak in the next stage from 20 to 30 years after graduation. If the engineer has been successful and accomplished their career goals, they are usually in a senior level technical or business leadership position, making significant contributions to the company's success. They are the upper level leaders determining the technical approaches and directing the engineering workforce. They are doing many career actions simultaneously, running departments, returning for training, mentoring junior people, and continuing their leadership development.[26]

Environmental engineers who are in the later stages of their careers might also wish to share their knowledge and experience through teaching, writing books, or publishing articles. Some quit their firms and become self-employed consultants, helping clients comply with regulations and complete cleanup operations at hazardous waste sites. Although some consultants earn more than those who work at large engineering firms, many environmental engineers do not look favorably on self-employment. Most prefer the security and benefits associated with working for an established company, and in 2016 only 2.7 percent of environmental engineers were self-employed.

> "If the engineer has been successful and accomplished their career goals, they are usually in a senior level technical or business leadership position, making significant contributions to the company's success."[26]
>
> —John A. Hoschette, engineering career consultant

Other Job Prospects

It is increasingly rare for an environmental engineer to stay at the same firm for decades. Environmental engineers might find themselves unemployed for reasons beyond their control. Companies downsize or close, and government agencies cut budgets and lay off workers. Other times environmental engineers seek new opportunities when they feel that they have reached a career dead end in which they are not learning and growing. Those who need or desire new employment opportunities have several career options.

Environmental engineers have many technical skills that can be used in civil engineering. Both professions design plans for various structures, and environmental engineers often work closely with civil engineers. For example, when a highway is built, a civil engineer might design the roadbed, bridges, and overpasses while the environmental engineer provides advice about issues concerning sewers, drainage, and water supplies. While both types of engineer earn about the same median wage, there are about five times more jobs in civil engineering, as engineering professor Gary Spring explains: "There is always a need for infrastructure improvements."[27]

Some environmental engineers use their education and experience to seek employment as chemical engineers. Engineers in both fields use chemistry, biology, physics, and math to solve problems. But chemical engineers use that knowledge to devise safe production methods for fuels, paints, plastics, chemicals, and drugs. Oftentimes companies that make chemical-based products work to institute production methods that are ecologically sound, and they seek engineers with an environmental background. In 2016 the annual median wage for chemical engineers was about $14,000 higher than that of environmental engineers.

The occupation of natural science manager is one of the most lucrative fields open to environmental engineers. Natural science managers combine their scientific skills with good management practices to supervise the work of chemists, physicists, biologists, and other scientists. They oversee research and development and coordinate production in laboratories, manufacturing plants, and research facilities. In 2016, the annual median wage for a natural science manager was $119,850, nearly $35,000 more than the median wage earned by an environmental engineer.

Wherever environmental engineers work, they use their training to create extremely detailed plans for systems that will function flawlessly for years. Those who apply the same kind of detailed analysis to their professional lives can create a career roadmap filled with opportunities. While they might face stiff competition along the way, those who invest the time and energy can earn a better wage and find greater job satisfaction as they work their way from junior engineer to senior-level technical expert.

CHAPTER 6

What Does the Future Hold for Environmental Engineers?

Nearly every day the news media report on environmental problems that are creating challenges around the world. Choking smog, polluted drinking water, toxic waste spills, and disasters associated with climate change are causing economic problems and human suffering. These problems are compounded by a rapidly expanding global population that requires new sources of sustainable freshwater and clean energy technology. Wherever the forces of nature are clashing with the needs of humanity, environmental engineers will be in great demand, as environmental scientist Matthew Mason explains:

> The future is likely to see . . . a greater need for enough food for our growing population, housing and facilities to cater to our growing needs, new farming methods and so on. . . . More areas [will require environmental] management to avoid pollution or ecological damage; we will see new potential contaminants as well as a need to change conditions in some areas to cope with the changing climate. There will be an even greater need for environmental engineers to help us deal with the potential problems that this future will bring.[28]

The expected need for more environmental engineers is reflected in numbers published by the Bureau of Labor Statistics (BLS). While overall job growth for all occupations is expected to grow by 7 percent through 2024, employment of environmental engineers is projected to increase by 12 percent, almost two times faster than the average. The field of environmental engineering is also growing more quickly than other engineering disciplines, which are only expected to grow by 4 percent through 2024.

Future Trends

The BLS predicts that job growth for environmental engineers will be stimulated as state and local governments search for ways to increase freshwater supplies. This need will be especially prevalent in arid western regions like Southern California, where environmental engineers have been designing, testing, and overseeing construction of desalination plants. These facilities can produce millions of gallons of freshwater every day by removing salt from ocean water. Some environmental engineers are working to create better filters and to design salt-removal systems. Others spend their days studying the environmental impact of desalination plants on ecologically fragile wetlands, beaches, and ocean waters where proposed facilities might be constructed.

> "There will be an even greater need for environmental engineers to help us deal with the potential problems that [the] future will bring."[28]
>
> —Matthew Mason, environmental scientist

The job demand for environmental engineers is also growing in the field of wastewater recycling technology. In 2017 environmental engineers were working on wastewater recycling facilities in Arizona, Texas, and New Mexico. And the job demand is not confined to the arid Southwest. The New York State Department of Labor projects job openings for environmental engineering technicians in the Finger Lakes region to rise by almost 29 percent through 2024. The Labor Department says demand will be fueled by state and local governments spending money to create more efficient water use and wastewater treatment systems.

Job Opportunities in the Green Building Industry

Designing sustainable structures, or so-called green buildings, is another predicted area of job growth for environmental engineers. The demand for energy- and water-efficient homes and offices is

Diversity Matters

In recent years engineering firms have been striving to add diversity to their workforces. This trend has resulted in a growing number of environmental engineering job openings for women, people of color, and the disabled. Women, who make up the fastest-growing sector of the environmental engineering field, are poised to take advantage of this move toward diversity. In 2016, 46 percent of the undergraduate degrees for environmental engineering went to women, compared with 19 percent for all engineering fields.

Engineering career consultant John A. Hoschette explains the benefits to environmental engineering firms that hire a more diverse workforce: "Having good options is what it is all about when faced with difficult engineering problems. A diverse team offers the potential to be more effective since its members can provide a wider variety of resources and solutions to the problem. With better solutions, the team is ultimately more efficient."

John A. Hoschette, *The Engineer's Career Guide*. Hoboken, NJ: John Wiley & Sons, 2010, p. 378.

growing. According to the 2016 *SmartMarket Report*, prepared by Dodge Research and Analytics, the economic impact of green building construction is expected to reach $234 billion in 2019. The market for retrofitting and renovating existing buildings is also expected to increase considerably. The United States Green Building Council (USGBC) predicts that commercial building owners will invest an estimated $960 billion globally in such renovation through 2023. These investments will help pay for environmental engineers to design and oversee the installation of renewable energy systems, water recycling systems, and other features that will make their structures sustainable. A similar trend is expected in the residential housing market.

The services of environmental engineers who specialize in software development are also expected to be in greater demand in the green building industry. Environmental software monitors and analyzes the performance of systems involved with producing solar and wind energy, purified water, and clean air. The software notifies consumers when maintenance is necessary and sends text messages with alert notices. According to the USGBC, new software management platforms will be added to 57 percent of all new commercial buildings and 56 percent of all new home construction and retrofit projects.

These developments translate into a thriving employment sector for environmental engineers who are working with sustainable building materials, zero-energy buildings, and next-generation solar energy systems. As engineer Michael Tobias explains,

> [During the next few years builders are] set to expand the use of green engineering innovations, and there's no doubt all building sectors will feel the surge. . . . Technology development and high performance will continue to protect human health and the environment. The emphasis will be on . . . [environmental] engineering processes to improve energy efficiency and renewable power generation.[29]

Some environmental engineers specialize in software development, particularly for use in the green building industry. This type of construction involves renewable energy and other sustainable practices.

New Jobs in Environmental Engineering

Job growth for environmental engineers is increasingly tied to exciting new innovations that are expected to generate employment in the coming years. For example, in 2017 a secretive research and development lab called X (and owned by Google) was hiring environmental engineers to develop cutting-edge technology. X engineers were designing, testing, and building high-altitude kite-like wind turbines for a project called Makani. The kites, with 85-foot (26 m) wingspans, fly high above the earth, where high wind speeds create an endless source of high-voltage electricity.

Agroforestry is another developing area for environmental engineers. Environmental engineers who specialize in agroforestry rely on their training in biology, ecology, agriculture, chemistry, and climatology. They use these skills to design site-specific land management systems that combine crops with beneficial shrubs and trees. Drought-resistant agroforestry sites produce food, medicinal plants, and textiles; provide wildlife habitat; and eliminate the need for toxic farm chemicals. Although not widely practiced, the demand for agroforestry projects is expected to grow in developing nations as challenges posed by climate change reduce the effectiveness of traditional farming practices.

Rolling Back Regulations

The job trends look bright for environmental engineers. But environmental engineer Fatih Temiz questions the promising scenarios by telling an oft-repeated joke among those in his profession: "Environmental engineering has been the job of the future for 30 years."[30] What Temiz means is that experts have long been predicting that the escalating number of environmental problems will increase the demand for services performed by environmental engineers. But the earnest efforts of environmental engineers are often thwarted by weak regulations, hostile politicians, an apathetic public, and a steady stream of budget cuts to environmental programs.

These factors were highlighted in 2017 after Donald Trump became president of the United States. Trump signed executive orders to roll back dozens of environmental regulations put in place by his predecessor, Barack Obama. Trump appointed Scott Pruitt, the former attorney general of Oklahoma, to head the EPA. Pruitt spent his career fighting environmental laws that regulate the oil and chemical industries. One of his early actions at the EPA was to repeal the Clean Power Plan, which was aimed at cutting carbon dioxide emissions from coal-fired power plants. In addition, Trump proposed cutting the EPA's budget by 31 percent while eliminating nearly fifty of the agency's programs. As a result of these actions, numerous environmental engineers quit their jobs at the EPA.

Only 6 percent of all environmental engineers work for the EPA and other federal agencies. But there is little doubt that the federal government will not be hiring many new environmental engineers at least through 2020. Additionally, as regulations that restrict emissions from power plants, oil producers, and other polluters are rolled back, these companies have less incentive to hire environmental engineers to keep them in compliance with the law. While this trend is distressing to some environmental engineers, Temiz remains an optimist: "Humanity is coming to its senses and will make a better future. . . . [When we someday travel to] Mars we'll need drinking water and need to dispose of our wastes and recycle everything. Who else but an environmental engineer is the best candidate for that? Even NASA needs environmental engineers."[31]

> "[When we someday travel to] Mars we'll need drinking water and need to dispose of our wastes and recycle everything. Who else but an environmental engineer is the best candidate for that?"[31]
>
> —Fatih Temiz, environmental engineer

Whatever the actions of the presidential administration, many corporate leaders understand that new investments in clean technologies will give the United States a competitive edge in the future. As each year passes, climate change is increasingly blamed for record-setting droughts, hurricanes, and wildfires. If there are answers to questions surrounding climate change and other environmental problems, they will likely be discovered by environmental engineers whose numbers will continue to grow regardless of the changes in the political climate.

Interview with an Environmental Engineer

Lashun Thomas has a doctorate in civil engineering with a focus on environmental and water resources. She has worked as an environmental engineer for eleven years and is the program co-ordinator for the environmental engineering program at the University of Arkansas at Little Rock. Thomas says she is one of the few women of color in the United States who oversee an environmental engineering program. She discussed her career during an interview with the author.

Q: Why did you become an environmental engineer?

A: I became an environmental engineer because I wanted to use my knowledge and skills to help change our world, to help change our environment, and to solve some of the challenging problems associated with making water cleaner and more available to those in need.

Q: What does an environmental engineer do?

A: As an environmental engineer, I develop innovative solutions to ensure that our environment will remain sustainable for generations to come. I focus on groundwater because it can specifically serve as a drinking water source, so it's important to be able to protect groundwater sources.

Q: Can you describe your typical workday?

A: When I'm studying groundwater issues, trying to look at the movement of subsurface waters, I work at a computer using groundwater modeling software. I may have to perform lab experiments, running lab tests on groundwater samples, especially if I'm worried about how clean the water is. For example, if I'm working on an environmental remediation project and have a chemical or pollutant that's in the groundwater, it's important for me to know the chemical composition of that compound and understand how it works when it's in the subsurface. And, if I'm looking at a remedial strategy that uses biological systems, I want to have some background on how the microorganisms will react when in contact with that particular pollutant. I can find answers and solutions to these problems by running samples in the lab.

Q: What do you like most about your job?

A: I have the opportunity to help people, to change lives, to directly impact the environment around us. And that's a wonderful feeling to be able to give back and to say I helped to bring clean water to that part of the country or that part of the world.

Q: What do you like least about your job?

A: You're not able in many cases to help everyone because of limited resources or limited funding. This may really hinder the amount of people you're actually able to help, and that's one of the things I would really like to do more of—I'd like to reach out and help more people.

Q: What personal qualities do you find most valuable for this type of work?

A: You have to be a determined person and also one who welcomes a challenge. It's really important to understand that environmental engineering is a very challenging career because you are directly accountable for the designs you propose and also any type of strategy that you offer as a potential solution. You have to be committed and hardworking. You have to be really willing to learn and be very open about choosing a new direction if your solutions do not pan out.

Q: What is the best way to prepare for this type of engineering job?

A: Have an appreciation for applied mathematics and many aspects of science. It's important that you have a grasp of chemistry, of physics, and also the biological systems as well. Because the work we do blends and integrates all aspects of those systems together. So you have to be able to utilize and leverage the knowledge and skills you learned in those fundamental areas.

Q: What advice do you have for students who might be interested in a career as an environmental engineer?

A: Read as much as you possibly can about environmental engineering and sciences and also be engaged in design. An engineer needs the ability not only to understand the scientific processes but also to design systems to fix problems. As an engineer, you're separated from scientists by the element of design. You're able to go to a different level when it comes to applying science to real-world problems.

Q: What specific advice do you have for female students and students of color interested in pursuing an environmental engineering career?

A: Just go for it. Just do it. In many cases you might be terrified to death and that's normal, but just take it one day at a time and keep moving forward. That's something I think you'll take with you throughout your lives and throughout your career. Females and women of color who graduate with engineering degrees commonly describe themselves as not being the smartest person in the room but as being the most dedicated and most committed person in the room. And that's different because when you're dedicated and committed to something, it can push you forward and lead you in the right direction.

SOURCE NOTES

Introduction: Engineering Everything

1. Quoted in Meghan Bogardus Cortez, "Q&A Christine Cunningham Proves Even Elementary Students Can Be Engineers," *EdTech*, June 19, 2017. https://edtechmagazine.com.

Chapter 1: What Does an Environmental Engineer Do?

2. Quoted in Tiree MacGregor, "Water Technology—a Growing Field," *Chronicle Herald* (Halifax, Nova Scotia), August 25, 2017. http://thechronicleherald.ca.
3. Quoted in Erika Ebsworth-Goold, "Engineers Work to Fight Pollution at Home, Globally," Washington University, August 11, 2017. https://source.wustl.edu.
4. Quoted in Integral Consulting, "Q&A with Craig Jones, Ph.D., Principal Ocean and Environmental Engineer," 2017. www.integral-corp.com.

Chapter 2: How Do You Become an Environmental Engineer?

5. Quoted in Cortez, "Q&A Christine Cunningham Proves Even Elementary Students Can Be Engineers."
6. Quoted in Cortez, "Q&A Christine Cunningham Proves Even Elementary Students Can Be Engineers."
7. Quoted in Quora, "What Do Mathematicians Really Think About Engineers?," June 2, 2016. www.quora.com.
8. Quoted in Quora, "I Want to Be Either a Civil Engineer or Environmental Engineer. What Are Things I Should Know?," November 13, 2016. www.quora.com.
9. Quoted in Quora, "How Do I Get an Environmental Engineering Internship?," April 26, 2016. www.quora.com.

Chapter 3: What Skills and Personal Qualities Matter Most—and Why?

10. G. Wayne Clough et al., "The Engineer of 2020," National Academy of Engineering, 2017. www.nap.edu.

11. Nader Mowlaee, "Top 23 Personality Traits of Ultra-successful Engineers," Interesting Engineering, July 12, 2017. https://interestingengineering.com.

12. 3DX, "7 Skills Needed to Be a Top Engineer," *3DConnexion* (blog), July 10, 2015. http://blog.3dconnexion.com.

13. Mowlaee, "Top 23 Personality Traits of Ultra-successful Engineers."

14. Quoted in Tekla S. Perry, "The Engineers of the Future Will Not Resemble the Engineers of the Past," *IEEE Spectrum*, May 30, 2017. https://spectrum.ieee.org.

15. Clough et al., "The Engineer of 2020."

16. Mowlaee, "Top 23 Personality Traits of Ultra-successful Engineers."

17. 3DX, "7 Skills Needed to Be a Top Engineer."

Chapter 4: What Is It Like to Work as an Environmental Engineer?

18. Quoted in Robin L. Flanigan, "Hot Job: Environmental Engineering Technician Fights Contamination in Rochester," *Rochester (NY) Democrat & Chronicle*, September 26, 2017. www.democratandchronicle.com.

19. Quoted in Flanigan, "Hot Job."

20. Quoted in DiscoverE, "What Engineers Do," 2017. www.discovere.org.

21. Quoted in LetsRun.com, "Environmental Engineers, What Is Your Day to Day Work Like?," March 3, 2013. www.letsrun.com.

22. Quoted in DiscoverE, "What Engineers Do."

23. John A. Hoschette, *The Engineer's Career Guide*. Hoboken, NJ: John Wiley & Sons, 2010, p. 137.

24. Quoted in DiscoverE, "What Engineers Do."

Chapter 5: Advancement and Other Job Opportunities

25. Quoted in DiscoverE, "What Engineers Do."

26. Hoschette, *The Engineer's Career Guide*, p. 24.

27. Quoted in Emmett Doerr, "5 Lucrative Engineering Careers and Career Paths," PayScale, 2017. www.payscale.com.

Chapter 6: What Does the Future Hold for Environmental Engineers?

28. Matthew Mason, "Why Environmental Engineering Is Vital to Our Future," Environmental Science, 2017. www.environmentalscience.org.
29. Michael Tobias, "The Top 10 Inventive Green Engineering Trends for 2017," *New York Engineers Blog*, New York Engineers, 2017. www.ny-engineers.com.
30. Quoted in Quora, "What Will Be the Future Job Market for Environmental Engineers?," August 18, 2017. www.quora.com.
31. Quoted in Quora, "What Will Be the Future Job Market for Environmental Engineers?."

Accreditation Board for Engineering and Technology (ABET)

415 N. Charles St.
Baltimore, MD 21201
www.abet.org

ABET accredits college and university programs in engineering and engineering technology at the associate's, bachelor's, and master's degree levels. ABET accreditation provides assurance that a college or university program meets the quality standards of the profession for which that program prepares graduates. The organization's website provides lists of ABET-accredited programs, information about attaining accreditation, and links to information about workshops and scholarships.

American Academy of Environmental Engineers and Scientists (AAEES)

147 Old Solomons Island Rd.
Annapolis, MD 21401
www.aaees.org

The AAEES provides training through workshops and seminars, participates in accrediting universities, publishes a periodical, and provides an educational network for students and young professionals. The academy's Student Team Awards recognize projects by college and university students.

Association of Environmental Engineering and Science Professors (AEESP)

1211 Connecticut Ave. NW
Washington, DC 20036
www.aeesp.org

The AEESP is made up of professors who teach environmental science and engineering courses that focus on water treatment, air pollution control, hazardous waste management, and related subjects. The association's website lists schools throughout the world that offer environmental engineering programs.

Engineers Without Borders

1031 Thirty-Third St., Suite 210
Denver, CO 80205
www.ewb-usa.org

Engineers Without Borders works in communities throughout the world to help them meet their basic water, energy, and food needs. Many of the volunteers are environmental engineering students who help install solar panels and sustainable water systems in rural villages. The organization has chapters on college campuses throughout the United States.

*Note: Boldface page
numbers indicate
illustrations.*

Accreditation Board
for Engineering and
Technology (ABET), 18,
23, 57
aerospace engineer, 6
Agency for International
Development, US, 35
agroforestry, 49
American Academy of
Environmental Engineers
and Scientists (AAEES),
42, 57
analytical skills, 25
Association of Environmental
Engineering and Science
Professors (AEESP),
57–58
awareness skills, 27–29
Axelbaum, Richard, 14–15

brownfields, 12–14
Bureau of Labor Statistics
(BLS), 37, 38, 45–46

carbon dioxide (CO_2)
emissions, 14
chemical engineer/
engineering, 18, 20, 44
Cheremeteff, Ari, 31, 32–33
civil engineer, 6, 44

Clean Power Plan, 50
climate change, 7, 14–15
Clough, G. Wayne, 24, 28
communication skills, 26
computer engineer, 6
Consortium for Clean Coal
Utilization, 14
cooperative education
programs (co-ops), 22
creativity, 28
Cunningham, Christine, 6,
17

Dare, Anne, 35
Department of Labor, New
York State, 46
desalination plants, 46
design, 34
diversity, in environmental
engineering field, 47
Dodge Research and
Analytics, 47

educational requirements,
4
bachelor's degree, 18–20
graduate degree, 20–22
high school courses,
17–18
Edwards, Marc, 5–6, 7
electrical engineer, 6
engineer
origin of term, 24
See also specific types

Engineering Is Elementary
  curriculum (Boston
  Museum of Science), 17
Engineers Without Borders,
  23, 58
entry-level positions, 38–39
Envirobot (robotic snake), 13
environmental engineer/
  engineering, **39**
  career ladder for, 38–41
  certification/licensing, **4**,
    23
  diversity in, 47
  educational requirements,
    4, 17–22
  entry-level positions in,
    38–39
  future trends in, 46, 49
  in green building industry,
    46–48
  growth rate in, **4**, 45–46
  impacts of deregulation
    on, 49–50
  information resources,
    57–58
  internships, 22
  interview with, 51–53
  job satisfaction and, 37
  salary/earnings, **4**, 38, 44
  skills/personal qualities, **4**,
    24
    operational skills, 25–27
    technical skills, 25
  working conditions, **4**
    company size and,
      36–37

fieldwork, 31–33, **32**
office work, 33–36
Environmental Protection
  Agency (EPA), 13, 50
environmental remediation,
  12–14, 31–33, 52
ethical standards, 29

fieldwork, 31–33
Flint (MI) water crisis, 5

Google, 49
gray water, 11
green building industry,
  46–48
groundwater pollution/
  remediation, 12, 19, 32,
  51–52

Hoschette, John A., 36, 41,
  42–43, 47
hydrogeology, 19
hydrologist, 8, **10**
hydrology, 19

ingenuity, 24, 28
internships, 22

Jha, Rajan, 34–35, 37
job satisfaction, 37
Jones, Craig, 15–16

Kamegai-Karadi, Tasha,
  40

Lu Engineers, 31–33

management, 42–43
Mason, Matthew, 45
mathematics, 17–18
mentors, 40, 41
modeling software, 34
Mowlaee, Nader, 25, 26, 29

National Academy of
  Engineering, 27–28
natural science manager, 44
Nixon, Jack, 17–18

Obama, Barack, 50
office work, 33–36
operational skills, 25–27

patents, 40
plane trigonometry, 18
Plummer, James, 26
pollution
  industrial, 6, 11–14, 31–33
Principles and Practice of
  Engineering exam, 23
professional engineer (PE)
  license, 23
Pruitt, Scott, 50

renewable energy, 7, 15
research teams, 22–23
Romero, Rachel, 33–34

salary/earnings, 38, 44
skills/personal qualities, **4**,
  24
  awareness skills, 27–29
  development of, 29–30

operational skills, 25–27
  technical skills, 25
SmartMarket Report (Dodge
  Research and Analytics),
  47
Snyder, Rick, 5
social issues
  awareness of, 27–29
software engineer, 6
solid waste engineering, 19
spherical trigonometry, 18
Spotter (solar-powered
  buoy), 15–16
Spring, Gary, 44
Stanford University, 21
statistics, 18

targeted brownfield
  assessment (TBA), 14
Taylor, Kerry-Anne, 9
team leaders, 28–29, 40–41
technical staff engineer,
  41–42
Temiz, Fatih, 49, 50
Thomas, Lashun, 51–53
Time (magazine), 5
Tobias, Michael, 48
tourist resorts
  infrastructure systems in,
  9–10
trigonometry, 18
Trump, Donald, 49–50

United States Green
  Building Council (USGBC),
  47, 48

University of California,
Berkeley (UCB), 21
*U.S. News & World
Report* (magazine),
21, 37

Vreeman, Fred, 18

wastewater management,
6–7, 9

wastewater recycling
technology, 46
water treatment plants, 8–9
wave energy, 15
Wouters, Frank, 22

X (research and
development lab), 49

Zaidel, Nicole, 33

PICTURE CREDITS

ABOUT THE AUTHOR

Stuart A. Kallen is the author of more than 350 nonfiction books for children and young adults. He has written on topics ranging from the theory of relativity to the art of electronic dance music. In addition, Kallen has written award-winning children's videos and television scripts. In his spare time, he is a singer, songwriter, and guitarist in San Diego.